ONE LOVE, GHOEMA BEAT

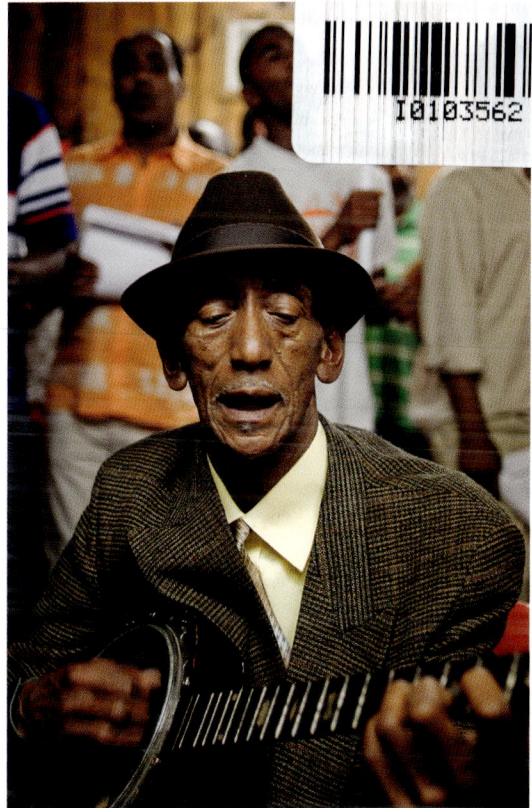

ONE LOVE, GHOEMA BEAT

Inside the Cape Town Carnival

photographs and text by

John Edwin Mason

UNIVERSITY OF VIRGINIA PRESS
CHARLOTTESVILLE

A volume in the series
Reconsiderations in Southern African History

First published in 2010 by Struik Travel & Heritage
(an imprint of Random House Struik (Pty) Ltd)
80 McKenzie Street, Cape Town 8001
P.O. Box 1144, Cape Town 8000, South Africa
Company Reg. No. 1966/003153/07
www.randomstruik.co.za

This paperback edition published by:
University of Virginia Press
P.O. Box 400318
Charlottesville, VA 22904–4318
USA

Publisher: Claudia Dos Santos
Managing editor: Roelien Theron
Editor: Patricia Myers Smith
Designer: Pete Bosman
Proofreader: Sean Fraser

Reproduction by Resolution Colour
Printed and bound by Kyodo Nation Printing Services Co., Ltd

ISBN 978-0-8139-3059-6
10 9 8 7 6 5 4 3 2 1

Cataloging-in-Publication data is available from the Library of Congress

HALF-TITLE PAGE The late Henry 'Gapie' van Aswyk rehearses with

the choir of the Pennsylvanians Crooning Minstrels.

TITLE SPREAD A Pennsylvanians band member warms up before an

inter-troupe competition.

RIGHT The Pennsylvanians sing and dance through the streets of

Hanover Park on their way to an inter-troupe competition.

contents

THIS SPREAD LEFT Members of the Spectacular Elsies Entertainers during a competition at the Vygieskraal Stadium. ABOVE LEFT A young member of the Pennsylvanians Crooning Minstrels. ABOVE RIGHT Faick Fredericks, the Pennsylvanians' senior drum major, leads the troupe down Darling Street during the *Tweede Nuwe Jaar* parade. OVERLEAF The choir of the Fabulous Woodstock Starlites competes at the Vygieskraal Stadium.

introduction

A minstrel troupe's *klopskamer* (clubhouse) can be a sleepy place, even in late December, only days away from the start of the Cape Town New Year's Carnival. On this warm summer afternoon in Hanover Park, a dusty, working-class coloured area in Cape Town's southern suburbs, the air is still and stifling. Members of the Pennsylvanians Crooning Minstrels, one of the Carnival's largest and most successful troupes, slowly trickle into the *klopskamer*, anticipating the evening's band rehearsal. Cars and *bakkies* (pick-ups) pull into the parking lot in front of the low, flat-topped building. Their occupants gather in small clusters to share a joke and a cigarette. In the front room, women work on the flowers and rosettes that will adorn the troupe's uniforms, while men talk and children play. From the back, the sweet, spicy aroma of *breyani* (a rice dish) floats out of a kitchen large enough to feed hundreds. In the furthest corner of the *klopskamer*, the senior members of the Pennsylvanians, all of them men, have a drink and assess the state of the troupe.

It soon becomes clear, however, that the day is winding up, not down. Band members slowly fill the rehearsal room, children first, followed by the grown-ups. Snatches of melody from a lonely trumpet are joined by the blare of trombones and the wail of saxophones. A cacophony of sound envelops the room and is studiously ignored by everyone who's not in the band. Even the arrival of the bandmaster fails to spark much interest. The melodies are recognisable now, but everybody knows that something is missing. That something is *ghoema*, the beating heart of Carnival. The music doesn't really begin until it arrives.

Ghoema is a drum, a pulse and, some would say, a way of life. Its roots lie deep in the history of Cape Town and in the history of the people who created Carnival and keep it alive. Ancestors of the coloured people, the community from which the minstrel troupes draw virtually all of their members, invented the drum and its rhythms. For Cape Town's servants and slaves in the eighteenth and nineteenth centuries, *ghoema* was a symbol of life in the face of exile and oppression. After slavery, it came to symbolise cultural independence and continuity in the midst of segregation and apartheid. *Ghoema* – the drum, the rhythm and the sensibility – provided the foundation on which the culture that gave birth to Carnival was built.

When the drummers arrive at the *klopskamer*, they aren't thinking about history or symbolism. Their minds are focused on this year's Carnival – the massive parade through the city centre on *Tweede Nuwe Jaar* (Second New Year, 2 January), the countless impromptu street marches through Cape Town's working-class coloured neighbourhoods, and the inter-troupe competitions that will last well into February.

Carnival's music and fellowship lift troupe members out of their ordinary routines and take them to a place where the hardships of daily life can be momentarily forgotten. But Carnival is also serious business, and the minstrel troupes are fiercely competitive. The Pennsylvanians, for instance, take great pride in their spirit, showmanship and status as Champion of Champions, a title they've earned 10 years in a row. The drummers, like everyone else in the troupe, understand that it won't be easy to retain the crown. Dozens of other troupes are eager to snatch it away. The drummers carry much of the burden of keeping the Pennsylvanians on top, for a troupe is only as good as its band, and a band is only as good as those who keep the *ghoema* beat.

As the sun sets and the air cools, the drummers begin the quick *dum-da-dum-dum* of *ghoema*. The atmosphere is transformed; there's fairy dust in the air. Old men, young girls, and those in between drop what they're doing and begin to dance. Others crowd into the room to get as close to the music as possible. Men and boys playing the *ghoema* drum (commonly called a *gamie*) are at the centre of the percussion corps. They are augmented by a bass drum and a tom-tom. More essential to the *ghoema* beat, however, are the traditional tambourines, which are made of animal skins stretched over round wooden frames; the shakers, which add a metallic shimmer to the sound; and the banjos, which, oddly enough, were borrowed from American blackface minstrelsy more than a century ago. Trumpets, trombones, and saxophones throw themselves into the mix, with the younger musicians playing music they've learned by rote and some of the older ones improvising over them. Rhythms, melodies and counter-melodies swirl around each other and then coalesce into a magnificent musical *bredie* (stew).

On days when the *ghoema* has been especially well prepared – and this is one of those days – the musicians and the rest of the troupe spill out of the *klopskamer* into the parking lot, and from there into the streets of Hanover Park. As the sky darkens, the band marches through the neighbourhood. People fall in behind it, singing and dancing; children pretend they're playing drums and trumpets with the band. This is the Pennsylvanians' gift to their friends and neighbours, a taste of the Carnival to come.

— |◘| —

In December 2007, I was lucky enough to have been a part of the scene I've just described. It was near the beginning of the second of three Carnival seasons I spent with the Pennsylvanians. (I also got to know several other troupes quite well, especially the Fabulous Woodstock Starlites.) I'm exceedingly grateful to Richard Stemmet, the owner of the Pennsylvanians, for allowing me to become, in effect, a member of his troupe.

As an 'honorary member' of the Pennsylvanians, I was an outsider with an insider's point of view. That perspective allowed me to document the Carnival in a way that has perhaps never been done before, exploring both its public and private sides. Public events, such as the great parade through central Cape Town on *Tweede Nuwe Jaar*, are important parts of this story. Readers of Cape Town newspapers will have seen many photos of the parade, though not from the perspective I offer – from within the troupe, not from the sidelines. Various inter-troupe competitions are held in local football stadiums throughout January and February. While these events attract many thousands of spectators, few people outside Cape Town's coloured community know about them. This book also looks at other aspects of Carnival that outsiders rarely see – such as band and choir rehearsals, life in the *klopskamers*, and the making of costumes and drums, among others. The result is a uniquely comprehensive look at the minstrel troupes.

I'm indebted to my friend Zane Ibrahim for getting me involved with the Carnival and opening the door to the Pennsylvanians. He knew that I'd written extensively about Cape Town's history and had adopted the city as a second home. When he realised, much to his dismay, that I had never seen so much as a single Carnival event, he immediately set out to rectify the situation. He spoke to Stemmet (Zane's family has been a part of the Pennsylvanians and their predecessors for over 50 years), and the troupe welcomed me like a long-lost cousin.

Initially, I thought that I would join the band. I have played the French horn in bands and orchestras since high school, and so I imagined the Carnival would throw nothing at me that I couldn't handle. I couldn't have been more wrong.

At my first band rehearsal, in December 2006, I instantly realised I was in trouble. The music was much more complex than I had anticipated, and it was memorised, not written down. It would have been nearly impossible for me to learn it all in the 10 days before Carnival began. Just as importantly, I couldn't quite master the *ghoema* beat. This is a very particular musical language, as unique as the jazz of New Orleans or the samba of Rio de Janeiro. Like all languages, it can be learned, but, unless one is born into the culture, fluency doesn't come easily. For me, it clearly wouldn't have come in time for Carnival.

So I put down my horn and picked up my camera. Thus this project was born.

While this book focuses on the minstrel troupes, it is important to note that there is much more to Carnival than the *klopse* (minstrels). The Malay Choirs, whose otherworldly singing blends European, Asian and African influences, are also an essential part of the Carnival. The choirs, in their guise as *nagtroepe* (night troupes), usher in each new year by parading through the central city on New Year's Eve. Christmas Bands, composed of brass and woodwind instruments, banjos and drums, march along the same route in mid-December to the sound of carols and hymns. On Christmas Eve, they perform their repertoire before their neighbours in the working-class coloured areas of the Cape Flats – sprawling, impoverished suburbs to which apartheid relegated coloureds and Africans. Like the minstrel troupes, the choirs and bands compete against each other during the early months of the year.

While the troupes, choirs and bands have distinctly different performance styles (the choirs and bands, dressed soberly in jackets and ties, are comparatively restrained), they are related to each other in a variety of ways. All draw their members almost entirely from the coloured community of Cape Town and the Western Cape, and memberships often overlap. It is not unusual for, say, a trumpeter to join both a minstrel band and a Christmas band. Many Malay choir members spend New Year's Eve marching through the city with their *nagtroep*, and then, with a change of costume, spend New Year's Day and *Tweede Nuwe Jaar* as *klopse*. In addition, much, though by no means all, of the music of all three organisations is built on the *ghoema* beat. Denis-Constant Martin, the great historian of the Carnival, calls *ghoema* the 'common thread' that binds together all the music of Carnival.

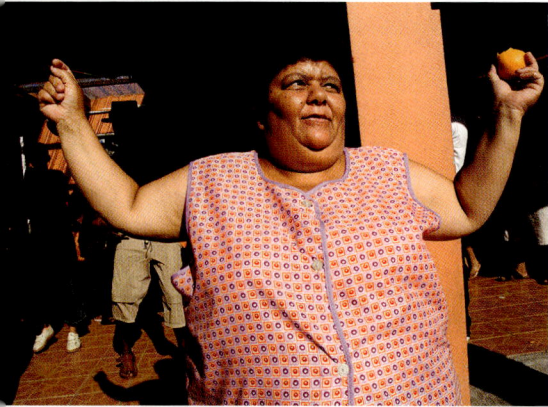

TOP Merle Jones dances to the *ghoema* beat during band rehearsal at the Pennsylvanians' *klopskamer*.
ABOVE A minstrel is ready for a competition.
RIGHT A member of the Pennsylvanians carries the South African flag past the old Slave Lodge (now a museum) in Adderley Street. Every *Tweede Nuwe Jaar*, the parade passes the lodge, linking Carnival's origins in the slave past to its new South African present.

Tweede Nuwe Jaar

'Dis **onse** dag!' ('This is **our** day!') —

TALIEP PETERSEN, IN 'RECOLLECTIONS OF NEW YEAR! NUWE JAAR!' (PART 1),
A TALIEP PETERSEN PRODUCTION, PRODUCED FOR SABC2 BY FREMANTLE PRODUCTIONS SA, 2007

It's 2 January, *Tweede Nuwe Jaar*. A brilliant sun is almost directly overhead, casting small pools of shadow at the feet of anyone brave enough to stand in its glare, and, as usual, Cape Town is a bundle of contradictions. In large areas of the city, it's business as usual as people go back to their pre-holiday routines. The working-class coloured neighbourhoods of the Cape Flats, however, are alive with the frenzied activity of tens of thousands of *klopse* as they don their costumes, paint their faces, and prepare for their annual parade through the central city. There, in the heart of Cape Town, many thousands of people crowd the pavements of Keizersgracht and Darling, Adderley and Wale streets, waiting for the parade to begin. Yet the streets themselves are oddly empty – there's not a minstrel to be seen or drum to be heard.

On the pavements, those in the know, who are mostly local and mostly coloured, have come prepared with blankets and fold-up chairs, cool drinks and snacks. They have been waiting for hours and will happily wait hours more. Others, mainly Carnival novices, looked at the schedule in newspapers, believed that festivities would start as advertised at 10 a.m., and are now growing restless. This happens every year. The Carnival runs on *klopse*-time.

Members of the Young Ones Youth Development troupe on Darling Street.

Spectators hear the troupes before they see them. The sounds of the *gamies* and voices of the *klopse* are faint and isolated at first, but build quickly as fleets of smoke-belching transit busses ferry members of Cape Town's more than 60 minstrel troupes into the central city. The troupes assemble above the city centre, on the street named Keizersgracht, which runs through what was once District Six, the old, racially mixed neighbourhood that apartheid destroyed. It's fitting that Carnival's most important event begins here, for District Six was, symbolically, the birthplace of both the Carnival and the coloured community.

At last the parade begins, hours late as far as city officials are concerned and right on time in the eyes of the *klopse*. Led by their junior and senior drum majors, their bands, their corps of little children, squadrons of dancers and sometimes their *moffies* (comically outrageous transvestites), legions of ordinary troupe members half-dance, half-march through their city, waving their umbrellas to the *ghoema* beat. For several hours, troupe after troupe, some of them nearly 1 000 members strong, surges past the ornate Victorian glory of the City Hall, through the office-block canyons of Adderley Street, past the gothic majesty of St George's Cathedral, and

up Wale Street hill into the Bo-Kaap, the 'Malay Quarter' of fading guidebooks. As the parade ends, the *klopse* board their waiting busses and head back to the Cape Flats, where they will spend much of the evening serenading their neighbours and having the time of their lives.

— ▣ —

The sights and sounds of the New Year's Carnival in Cape Town are remarkably similar to those of carnivals in Rio de Janeiro, New Orleans and Venice, as well as less well-known carnivals around the world. For thousands of years, carnivals have been times of ritualised disorder, when the rules of everyday life are momentarily suspended. Revelry and indulgence reign. Music, dance and feasting are the order of the day. The mighty are mocked, and the lowly take centre stage. The words of the old Carnival song that Cape Town's minstrels sing every year sum up the feeling: '*Dis 'n nuwe jaar, ons is deurmekaar.*' ('It's a new year, we're deliriously happy' – in cases such as this, any translation can only be approximate.)

Carnivals are also rites of renewal. In the broadest sense, they are annual celebrations of a community's survival and of the continuities between its past, present and future.

In pre-Christian Europe, carnivals took place in the spring, when the return of light and life, after the desolation of winter, enhanced a sense of rebirth. Carnivals in Europe and the Americas later acquired an additional layer of Christian meaning, with the festival's tradition of sensual excess becoming a prelude to the austerity of Lent.

Cape Town's Carnival, like carnivals everywhere, is a time of renewal and organised chaos, but it stands alone among the world's great carnivals in having nothing to do with the seasons of the northern hemisphere, nor with the cycle of the Christian calendar. (In fact, many members of the minstrel troupes, and virtually all members of the Malay Choirs, are Muslims.) This carnival is the unique creation of Cape Town's coloured community, and its roots are buried deep in their history and in the past of their city.

Ask any minstrel when the Carnival began and the answer you'll get is 'in slavery', nearly two centuries ago. *Tweede Nuwe Jaar*, you'll be told, was the slaves' own holiday, the only day of the year that they had to themselves. It was a time to visit family and friends, sing and dance to the beat of a drum, and be merry. When freedom finally came, in the 1830s, Emancipation Day just happened to fall on 1 December, very close to the festive season. Large groups of newly freed people, dressed in the finest clothes they could afford, marched through the streets in celebration. Commemorations of emancipation soon merged with the New Year's holiday. Here, it is commonly said, was Carnival in embryo: fancy dress, singing and dancing, parading … and the *ghoema*'s joyful beat.

The history of Cape Town's Carnival is more complicated than this popular version suggests. A more complete account of its origins would show how slowly it evolved over time – its rhythms, melodies and vocal inflections mirror Cape Town's polyglot culture, drawing on a variety of sources, especially Indonesia, Malaysia, Sri Lanka, India and East Africa, areas that supplied slaves to the Cape Colony in the seventeenth and eighteenth centuries. The costumes, face-painting and music of American blackface minstrelsy, which was a popular form of entertainment in late nineteenth-century Cape Town, also shaped Carnival. The troupes' marching parodies the military precision of nineteenth-century British garrisons, and a substantial portion of Carnival's songs originated in the Netherlands. Nevertheless, popular history tells us a good deal about what Carnival meant to the people who created it and means to those who now sustain it, especially when it is viewed as an allegory rather than a literal truth.

On *Tweede Nuwe Jaar*, the coloured working class, which survived slavery, segregation and apartheid, celebrates itself. As the late Taliep Petersen, Cape Town musician and composer, said, '*Dis **onse** dag*!' ('It's **our** day!'). When the *klopse* look at themselves, on their day, they see multitudes. Tens of thousands of minstrels and endless throngs of spectators – a vast sea of humanity, largely coloured. Certainly, there are significant numbers of whites sprinkled throughout, and occasionally African faces can be seen. Nevertheless, John Western's observation, made more than two decades ago, remains true today: Carnival is 'one of the few **specifically** coloured aspects of Cape Town cultural life' (*Outcast Cape Town*, Human & Rousseau, 1981, p. 146).

The Carnival is more than a celebration. It is also a homecoming. In the popular imagination, District Six, which bordered central Cape Town, was both the birthplace of Carnival and home to the the coloured community. The Group Areas Act, a grotesque piece of apartheid-era legislation designed to make South African cities lily white, literally destroyed District Six. The Act drove 150 000, mostly coloured, people out of Cape Town's mixed neighbourhoods and into the featureless wasteland of the Cape Flats. District Six, once home to 60 000 and bulldozed in the 1970s, is widely viewed as representative of these forced removals, even though it was by no means the only affected area in the city.

District Six was where the annual parade began before winding its way through the city, into the Bo-Kaap and on to Green Point, where the earliest competitions were held more than a century ago. After driving coloured people out of District Six and other parts of Cape Town, the apartheid authorities tried to rid the city of Carnival as well. The parade on *Tweede Nuwe Jaar* occurred only sporadically during the apartheid years; permission to march came grudgingly, if at all.

Seen in this light, the return of the Carnival troupes to District Six on *Tweede Nuwe Jaar,* and their march through central Cape Town, has great symbolic significance. It is an effort by the Group Areas Diaspora to rewrite history. Every 2 January, they create an ideal, if imaginary, Cape Town – a Cape Town without apartheid and forced removals, without exclusion and humiliation. For a brief moment in time, the city is restored, the community is made whole, and the wounds of the past are healed.

Devilish figures are very much a part of Carnival, much to the delight of the children they pretend to chase.

LEFT The Pennsylvanians' junior drum major, Nathan Carolus, relaxes before leading the troupe down Darling Street.

ABOVE The parade always brings out the press – images of the Carnival will crowd the next day's newspapers.

OPPOSITE Nathan Carolus, the Pennsylvanians' junior drum major. ABOVE Banjos and tambourines have been part of Carnival bands for well over 100 years, but the banjo's glory days may be fading – few young people want to learn how to play it.

The parade on *Tweede Nuwe Jaar* ends with an uphill climb on Wale Street, but the hill rarely slows anybody down.

The Pennsylvanians' senior drum major, Faick Fredericks, waits for the parade to begin, as spectators occupy every millimetre of the pavement and crowd the ramparts and walls of the Castle of Good Hope.

On Adderley Street, a statue of Jan Christiaan Smuts, a former prime minister, offers a vantage point for Carnival fans.

Every troupe has a 'board', which is carried proudly during parades and competitions. Boards are usually made by specialists and represent a considerable investment. Here the Hollywood Superstars' board honours former president Nelson Mandela.

A troupe nears the end of the parade, crossing Buitengracht Street and entering the Bo-Kaap, one of the old neighbourhoods in which Carnival traditions were born.

A troupe's band crosses Buitengracht Street.

Cell phones may not be a part of Carnival's traditions, but troupe members can't seem to put them down, especially on *Tweede Nuwe Jaar*.

The music and dance of Carnival can sometimes induce an ecstatic, almost trance-like state. Troupe members refer to it as *tarik*.

World events and the Carnival collide in 2007.

In 2009, the board and banners of the Atlantis Community Entertainers celebrate the recent election of Barack Obama as president of the United States. Many people in South Africa's coloured community identify strongly with African-Americans and greeted Obama's election with joy.

A member of the Atlantis Community Entertainers flies the American flag in 2009 in honour of Barack Obama's recent election as United States president.

The colonial past meets the democratic present, as members of the Pennsylvanians Crooning Minstrels march past Cape Town's City Hall.

Zane Ibrahim, a veteran member of the Pennsylvanians, keeps the beat as spectators watch the troupe march down Darling Street.

In contrast to Rio de Janeiro's Carnival and the Mardi Gras in New Orleans, women and girls in Cape Town's Carnival dress modestly, usually wearing the same uniforms as men and boys. These costumes are unusually skimpy.

The drums in the foreground and centre are *gamies*, the beating heart of Carnival.
Its music and rhythms are unimaginable without them.

Moffies – comically outrageous cross-dressers – have been a part of the topsy-turvy world of Carnival for many years. Most people heartily approve, but some, it seems, are more sceptical.

The Pennsylvanians' band marches up Adderley Street. The troupe is one of several that offers free instruments and music lessons to local youth.

Cecil 'Doupie' Waterloo enjoys a break during the *Tweede Nuwe Jaar* parade.

Backstage at the Carnival

Moegammad Cassiem – everybody calls him 'Monte' – is one of the busiest tailors in Cape Town, but you won't find his shop in the city's commercial district or in one of the shopping malls that dot the Cape Flats. He's also not the guy you would go to for a sports coat or a wedding gown. Monte's workshop is in his home on the Flats, and his business is making the uniforms for Cape Town's minstrel troupes.

Each Carnival troupe requires an entirely new set of uniforms every year. Monte works for 8 to 10 troupes each season, turning out as many as 10 000 individual outfits. He can't do this by himself. When I drop by to see him, in late December, the house is overflowing with men, women and machines, and every square metre of floor space seems to be covered by an endless rainbow of brightly coloured cloth. In the garage, three or four men wielding industrial cutters are using battered cardboard patterns to turn bolts of fabric into the arms, legs, shoulders and lapels of minstrel uniforms. In the house itself, five or six seamstresses, hunched over ancient black sewing machines, float like islands in a sea of partially assembled gear. Back in the kitchen Monte is negotiating with a couple of troupe leaders who are demanding more uniforms than they'd originally ordered, but have brought neither cloth nor cash, both of which are essential to the task.

The workshop of Achmat Sabera – known to one and all as 'Boeta Achmat' – is further out on the Cape Flats. He's one of the city's finest woodworkers, and his shop, like Monte's, is in his home. He's been blessed with an eye that can unfailingly find the beauty hidden in the roughest

Moegammad 'Monte' Cassiem, one of the Carnival's busiest tailors, examines a new uniform in his home workshop, while his daughter looks on.

wood and with hands that have the skill to reveal it. But you won't find any of his magnificently crafted creations in a boutique or a gallery. Boeta Achmat makes *gamies* and tambourines for the Carnival.

Even now, a day or two before the Carnival begins, Boeta Achmat's house is an oasis of serenity. When I first met him, he had recently returned from a pilgrimage to Mecca, and the sense of calm and repose that surrounded him then lingered on. His wife, Gadija, operates a small tuck shop out of the front room. Occasionally, she rises to sell a cool drink or packet of chips to teenagers who knock on the front door, but, as always, she has time to offer me a cup of tea. Boeta Achmat leads me through the kitchen and into his back yard to show me *gamies* and tambourines in various stages of completion. It's a process that can't be hurried – skins for the heads of the drums and tambourines must be tanned; wood must be soaked in water before it can be bent; lacquer must dry. Boeta Achmat, in any case, is not someone who will be rushed. Every drummer in the Carnival wants to play one of his instruments, and each of them knows to order early or not at all.

Several kilometres to the south, in the Hanover Park *klopskamer* of the Pennsylvanians Crooning Minstrels, the band and choir are putting some of Boeta Achmat's drums and tambourines to good use. With only a few days of rehearsal time remaining before the first competition of the year, Ahmad Ismael, the Pennsylvanians' choir director (who is called a 'coach'), isn't happy with what he's hearing. He stops to correct every mistake; even the smallest flaw can mean the difference between winning and losing.

In lower Woodstock, one of the few coloured areas near the central city to have escaped forced removals, the Fabulous Woodstock Starlites are also hard at work. Their choir, accompanied by a virtual band loaded onto the hard drive of a laptop computer, practises long into the night. It will be nearly midnight when the singers, sustained only by many cups of hot, sweet tea, join the rest of the troupe to practise marching manoeuvres in the narrow streets.

— |◦| —

Throughout the latter part of the year, and especially in October, November and December, scenes like these are re-enacted all over the Cape Flats and in the more central working-class coloured areas. Some 60 minstrel troupes are preparing for the Carnival. Perhaps a dozen tailors, including

Monte, have hired cutters and seamstresses to help them in the mad scramble to finish between 400 and 1 000 uniforms for each troupe. (A few, such as the Starlites, make their own, relying on the labour of female members.) One or two drum- and tambourine-makers are trying, and failing, to match the quality of Boeta Achmat's instruments.

Few outsiders realise that minstrel troupes are active throughout the year. A number of troupes sponsor a youth band that practises one or two days a week all year long. Trumpets, saxophones, trombones, clarinets and free instruction are provided to children who wish to join. The Pennsylvanians see this as a way both to strengthen their band and to offer youngsters an alternative to drugs, gangs and the street. Like the bands, the choirs begin to rehearse when Carnival season is a distant dream. By their very presence, the bands and choirs bring the *klopskamers* to life, attracting troupe members who want to listen or simply hang out with their friends. During July and August the troupes hold Winter Balls, at which members and their friends drink, feast and dance into the small hours of the morning.

Even at the height of the season, there are aspects of Carnival that are hidden in plain sight. For instance, before arriving in central Cape Town for the parade on *Tweede Nuwe Jaar*, or at one of the football stadiums for a competition, the troupes march through their neighbourhoods (and often other areas as well) in full regalia, with their bands leading the way. Sometimes they stop at a particular house, put on a show and are offered a *tafel* (table) of melons, biscuits and cool drinks for their efforts.

These activities are aspects of Carnival's private side, and, for troupe members, they're every bit as significant and pleasurable as the great parade on *Tweede Nuwe Jaar* and the inter-troupe competitions. Few *klopse*, for example, view the rehearsals as burdens. These are voluntary associations, after all, and anyone who's disgruntled simply stops showing up. Everyone knows that no troupe can sound or look sharp without dedication. Just as importantly, the rehearsals and balls are ways of making the feeling of Carnival last as long as possible. As a troupe member once told me, 'Carnival is our holiday. We don't have houses by the sea. We don't fly away to Paris. This is all we have.'

None of this is to deny that Carnival does impose burdens, many of them financial. Most troupes pay their expenses out of their own pockets. A few of the larger and more successful ones, such as the Pennsylvanians, have corporate sponsorship, and the city and provincial government lend a hand to the associations that organise the competitions. But these subsidies never come close to covering all of a troupe's expenses, which include buying cloth for costumes, providing instruments for the band (if the troupe has its own), hiring a band (if it doesn't) and paying for tailors, vocal soloists, a coach for the choir and busses to transport the troupe to the city centre and to the stadiums.

The task of finding the money falls first and foremost to the troupe's 'owner' or 'captain'. He or she is typically a skilled artisan or successful small business owner. On rare occasions, one has to admit, the owner is a gangster. As is the case with the samba schools of Rio, running a minstrel troupe is an expensive proposition. In Rio's impoverished *favelas* and in the working-class coloured suburbs of the Cape Flats, those with money have sometimes acquired it illegally. Most troupe owners, whether crooked or straight, grew up in a Carnival family and, after some years as a member of someone else's troupe, decided to start one of their own. While any new troupe owner has to be prepared to invest deeply in upfront costs, he or she usually has help from the troupe's 'committee', made up of senior members who help to manage and fund the troupe's activities. Individual members purchase their uniforms from the troupe's owner, paying R200 to R300 per uniform. In fact, the purchase of a uniform (troupe members call it their 'gear') is the most important act of becoming a member of a troupe. Anyone who wants to be a member of the band or choir or to take part in the Grand March Past and Exhibition March during competitions must attend rehearsals. But if one's goal is simply to join in the merriment on *Tweede Nuwe Jaar*, buying the gear means that one has joined the troupe.

Like the banjo and the top hat, face-painting is a tradition Cape Town minstrels borrowed from American blackface minstrelsy in the nineteenth century. Here, in a courtyard at their *klopskamer*, members of the Pennsylvanians prepare for the parade on *Tweede Nuwe Jaar*.

One of the leaders of the Pennsylvanians shows off the troupe's Winter Ball decorations.
The ball brightens an otherwise cold and rainy season.

At the Pennsylvanians' Winter Ball, tables will groan under the weight of samoosas, meat pies, salad, and a staggering variety of things to drink, while members, spouses and friends crowd the dance floor.

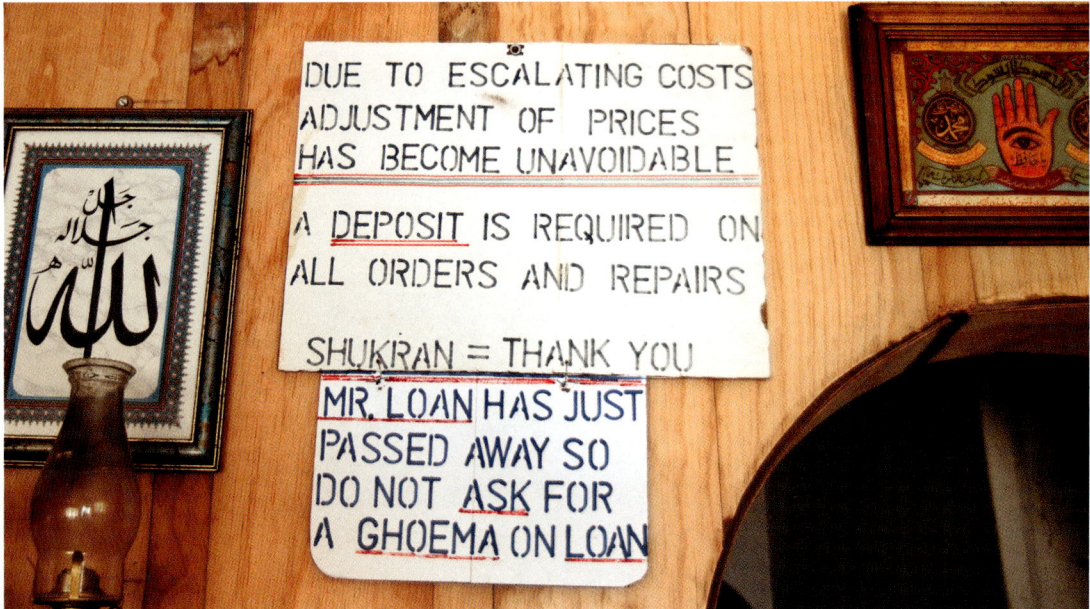

Signs on the wall of the home and workshop of Boeta Achmat Sabera, maker of extraordinary drums and tambourines.

Boeta Achmat nails the head on a *gamie*, in the workshop behind his home.

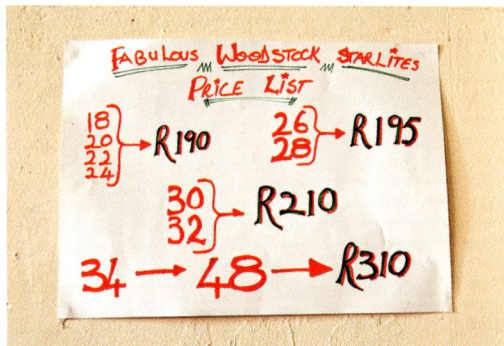

FABULOUS WOODSTOCK STARLITES
PRICE LIST

18
20
22
24 → R190

26
28 → R195

30
32 → R210

34 → 48 → R310

TOP A sign in the Fabulous Woodstock Starlites' rehearsal hall gives the prices of the year's uniform.

ABOVE Hats await their buyers in the Pennsylvanians' *klopskamer*.

RIGHT Cardboard patterns hang in Monte Cassiem's workshop.

Red Suits

**ACT UPON THEM
IN NUMERICAL ORDER**

Young T.V. Stars

1	40	— 32
2	60	— 34
3	60	— 36
4	60	— 38
5		— 40
6	5	— 42
7	5	— 44
8		

OPPOSITE The granddaughter of Monte Cassiem plays with a uniform hat, while a seamstress works in the background. ABOVE Boxes
of cloth and partially assembled uniforms surround one of the seamstresses working for Monte Cassiem.

A member of the Pennsylvanians Crooning Minstrels watches the band rehearse in the *klopskamer*.

During the Carnival season, a troupe's band never rehearses alone. Troupe members stop by to listen and, inevitably, dance to the *ghoema* beat, as here, in the Pennsylvanians' *klopskamer*.

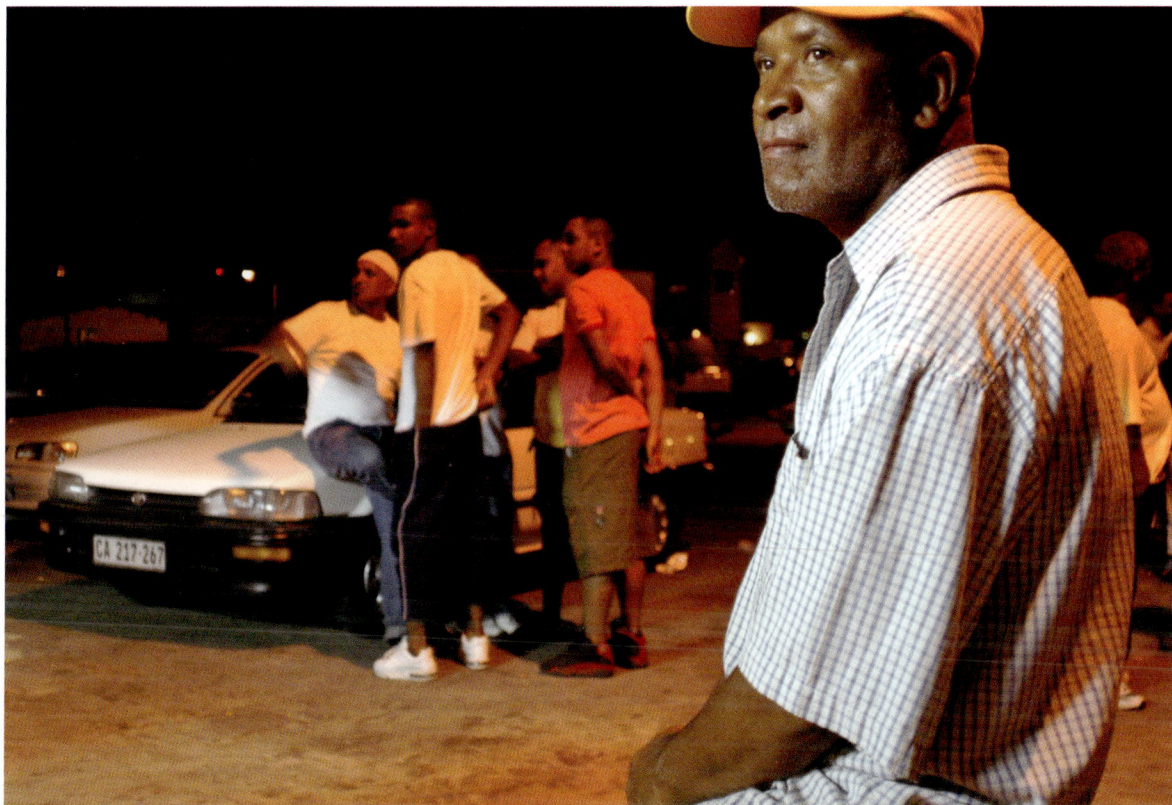

OPPOSITE Late on a summer's night, Fabulous Woodstock Starlites drummers beat out a cadence as the precision-marching team practises the Grand March Past. ABOVE A troupe's *klopskamer* provides members, such as the Pennsylvanians in this picture, with a place to enjoy each other's company.

ABOVE The Nokia All-Stars' choir rehearses in its *klopskamer* on a cold winter night.

RIGHT The choirs of every troupe work hard during their practices, and it's not always fun.

The Pennsylvanians Crooning Minstrels is one of several troupes that encourage young people to join the band, supplying them with instruments and instruction.

The Pennsylvanians' band rehearses in its *klopskamer*.

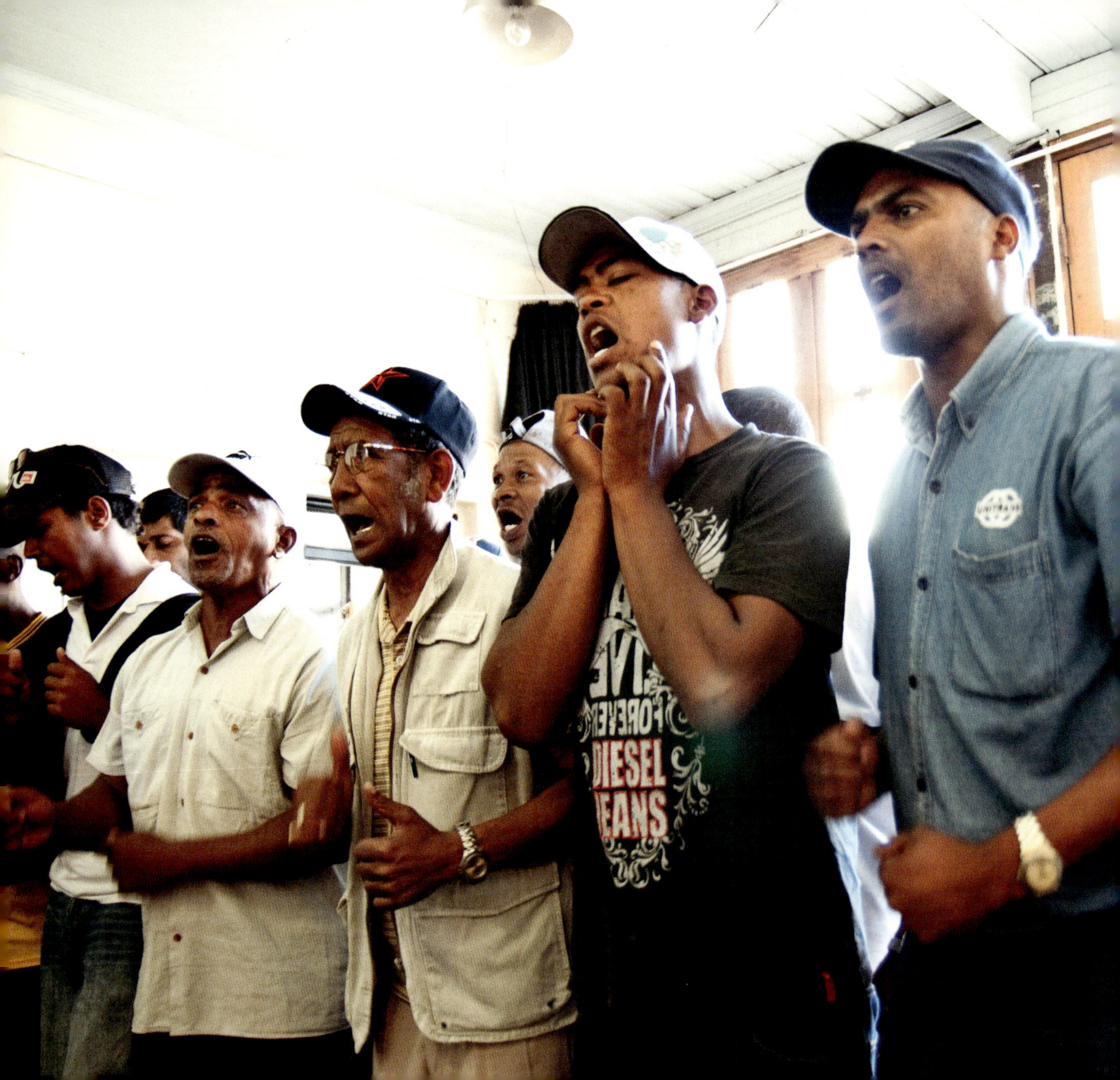
DIESEL

The choir of the Fabulous Woodstock Starlites practises in its rehearsal hall.
The musical accompaniment is prerecorded and played back via a laptop computer.

ABOVE AND BELOW, LEFT It may be only a rehearsal, but the Fabulous Woodstock Starlites' choir always puts a tremendous amount of energy into its singing. OPPOSITE Ahmed Ismail, who has led the Pennsylvanians' choir for many years with great success, conducts a rehearsal in the *klopskamer*.

Zane Ibrahim's family has been connected to the Pennsylvanians and
their predecessor troupes, in District Six, since the 1930s.

Children are introduced to the intricacies of *ghoema* at an early age, often by family members.

These boys are the sons, grandsons and nephews of other Pennsylvanians.

Women in the troupe or from the community make and sell the rosettes many minstrels buy to adorn their uniforms.

It's an important source of income for their families.

Joining the troupe offers young people an alternative to the street.

Face-painting is an art form that troupe members learn while they're still young, as here in the Pennsylvanians' *klopskamer*.

The top hat worn by the Pennsylvanians member on the right is a reminder of the ways in which American minstrelsy influenced the Carnival.

LEFT During the height of the Carnival season, members of the Pennsylvanians Crooning Minstrels face a tiring schedule of parades and competitions.

TOP Impromptu street marches through townships such as Manenberg delight local children.

ABOVE Troupes can expect to be thanked for their efforts with a *tafel* (table) of cool drinks, melons and curries.

A hastily organised street march through Manenberg attracts a large crowd.

The Pennsylvanians Crooning Minstrels' band in Manenberg.

You don't have to be a minstrel to love the *ghoema* beat.

A member of the Pennsylvanians rushes back to the *klopskamer* to catch a ride to a competition at the Athlone Stadium.

Young members of the Fabulous Woodstock Starlites play in a vacant lot, while waiting for the busses that will take the troupe to central Cape Town for the parade on *Tweede Nuwe Jaar*.

ABOVE The Fabulous Woodstock Starlites' band warms up. Any time a troupe's band begins to play, neighbourhood children appear.

OVERLEAF Jamaldien Jumah leads the Fabulous Woodstock Starlites through the streets of Woodstock, a working-class Cape Town neighbourhood.

OPPOSITE A corps of small children marches near the front of every troupe. ABOVE Each troupe has a member or two who is especially good at face-painting. This young member of the Fabulous Woodstock Starlites probably can't wait to see how she looks.

Champion of Champions

It's New Year's Day, 2007, and I'm with the Pennsylvanians Crooning Minstrels as they tumble out of their busses and onto the hot tar of the Green Point Stadium parking lot. I am in uniform and, except for the camera in my hand, indistinguishable from anyone else in the troupe. We'll soon enter the stadium to compete against over a dozen other troupes in the *Klopse Jol*, an event that determines, in essence, which troupe can best march and have a party at the same time. Despite the heat, spirits are high, laughter abounds and silliness runs rampant. Carnival has officially begun.

Within the overall atmosphere of exuberance, however, there are undercurrents of tension and anticipation. Like most troupes, the Pennsylvanians take the competitions seriously. All of us are well aware that our troupe is the reigning Champion of Champions. We have no intention of simply giving our crown away. While the *Klopse Jol* is by no means the most difficult of disciplines, the troupe must still deliver sights and sounds spectacular enough to impress the judges. With that in mind, we are glad to be wearing our new uniforms for the first time. The creases are crisp, and the colours are so dazzling that the white polka dots on our jackets seem ready to leap off their background of brilliant red.

If I'm more nervous than the others, it is only partly because this is my first outing as a member of the Pennsylvanians. I'm certainly hoping that I don't screw anything up, but it seems to me that if everyone else can simultaneously march and party, I ought to be able to march and take photographs. What really worries me is tripping over my uniform pants. When I bought my gear

A drum major leads his troupe into Vygieskraal Stadium for the Grand March Past, one of the most important events in the inter-troupe competitions.

and tried it on in the *klopskamer*, everything seemed fine. But the pants must have grown overnight. This morning they were much too long, and I spent a couple of hours trying to figure out a way to shorten them. I searched high and low in the furnished apartment I'm renting from my friends Alan and Cynthia, but couldn't find anything resembling a needle and thread. I did come across four safety pins and some electrical tape, and that is what's currently keeping my turn-ups from dragging along on the ground.

It is late afternoon when our turn comes to perform. As we approach the entrance to the stadium, a wave of nostalgia washes over the older members of the troupe. They know that this season's competitions may well be the last ever to be held in Green Point. The tradition of organised competitions began exactly 100 years ago, when the whites-only Green Point Cricket Club organised a 'coloured carnival' in an effort to raise funds for the club. The venue was the old Green Point Track, a bicycle racing facility, and the events – which included band and choir competitions and a 'Grand March Past' by entire troupes – were very similar to those of the competitions of today. Seven troupes participated in that first 'coloured carnival', and it was so successful (at raising money for the sports club, not the troupes) that another was held the following year.

Green Point Track and Green Point Stadium have been the arenas most identified with the Carnival ever since, even though competitions occurred only intermittently during the first half of the twentieth century and other stadiums have often been used. Now the old stadium has reached the end of its life. The Cape Town City Council has replaced it with a much larger modern structure in time for the 2010 Soccer World Cup™. No one knows whether the *klopse* will ever *jol* (party) in the new stadium. To anyone with a sense of history, it feels like the end of an era.

— ◖◗ —

The Carnival's inter-troupe competitions serve two purposes: to establish a pecking order among the minstrels and to extend the Carnival feeling. Judges, who are often from outside the coloured community, rate the troupes in particular events – band, choir and vocal soloist performances, plus the *Klopse Jol*, Grand March Past and Exhibition March Past. Winners of individual events earn a trophy; the troupe with the strongest average score is declared the overall

winner, the Champion of Champions. Winning an event, and especially winning the title, greatly enhances a troupe's prestige, allowing it to attract new members, including talented singers and musicians. A win also helps the group court corporate sponsorship.

The competitions allow troupe members to keep the spirit of Carnival alive for several weeks after the parade on *Tweede Nuwe Jaar*, just as band, choir and marching rehearsals do in the months preceding the New Year. Except for the opening competition on 1 January, the others are held on Saturdays during January and the first half of February, in stadiums packed with fans who have turned out to cheer for their favourites. The atmosphere is electric. The better troupes feed off this energy, producing performances that are far superior to anything seen or heard during rehearsals. The judges' decisions are final, but rarely popular. None of the minstrels and few of the fans will readily accept that their own troupe is anything but the best.

Every Cape Town New Year's Carnival ends late on a Saturday night in early February, when the troupe that is Champion of Champions carries the trophy off the field.

In a very real sense, Carnival begins the next day, when the owners and captains of the troupes start to plan for the following year and when ordinary *klopse* begin to dream.

Minstrels dance to the *ghoema* beat, outside the old Green Point Stadium.

PREVIOUS PAGE Young troupe members march in review during a competition at the Vygieskraal Stadium.

ABOVE Members of the Atja Indians compete at Vygieskraal.

The leader of the Atja Indians watches his troupe perform during a competition at the Vygieskraal Stadium. The Atjas' uniforms – a throwback to the early twentieth century, before minstrel uniforms became standardised – mimic Hollywood's version of Native American garb.

OPPOSITE The Atja Indians emphasise their fascination with Native American culture by marching with the American flag as well as the South African flag at the Vygieskraal Stadium. ABOVE A troupe's band performs at Vygieskraal during a competition.

ABOVE The Exhibition March Past, a major competition event, allows troupes to address pressing social issues, such as crime, drugs, xenophobia and HIV/Aids. OPPOSITE The setting sun shines through the misspelled banner of the Fabulous Woodstock Starlites at Vygieskraal Stadium.

The Pennsylvanians Crooning Minstrels perform the *Klopse Jol* during one of the last competitions to be held at the old Green Point Stadium.

ABOVE The colours minstrels pick for their face paint often reflect those of their uniforms.

OVERLEAF The setting sun illuminates a troupe's choir during a competition at the Vygieskraal Stadium.

ABOVE A member of the Pennsylvanians plays the tambourine as the troupe prepares for an evening of competition in the old Green Point Stadium.

RIGHT Ahmed Ismail leads the Pennsylvanians' choir during a competition at the Athlone Stadium.

A minstrel takes a rest at Athlone Stadium. A long day of street marches and competition takes its toll, even on the relatively young.

Ahmed Ismail leads the Pennsylvanians' choir in warm-up exercises before they compete at the Athlone Stadium.

The old Green Point Stadium was already being dismantled to make way for the new Cape Town Stadium when the Pennsylvanians' band competed there in 2007. The very first inter-troupe competition had been held nearby, at the Green Point Track, exactly 100 years earlier.

Vygieskraal Stadium always overflows with people during the Carnival competitions.

The competitions last well into the night.
Despite the late hour and chilly weather,
Vygieskraal Stadium is still packed.

ABOVE The Pennsylvanians' band competes before a large crowd at Athlone Stadium.

OPPOSITE In 2007, the Pennsylvanians were crowned overall winner – Champion of Champions – for the tenth consecutive year.

'Babbie'

Acknowledgements

Besides Richard Stemmet and Zane Ibrahim, there are many other people whom I must thank for helping to make this book possible.

First among equals is my friend Denis-Constant Martin. He's the author of *Coon Carnival: New Year in Cape Town, Past and Present* (David Philip, 1999). This publication is by far the most important scholarly study of the subject. My debt to him, both personal and intellectual, is enormous.

Jamaldien Jumah, owner of the Fabulous Woodstock Starlites, generously allowed me to spend time with his troupe, taking photographs and getting to know its members.

Vincent Kolbe, musician, historian and sage, has gladly shared with me his wisdom, laughter and enthusiasm for Cape Town ever since I appeared on his doorstep.

How Susie Newton-King has put up with my presence in her spare bedroom on and off for these many years is something I'll never understand, but for which I'll be eternally grateful.

I'm also grateful to Moegammad 'Monte' Cassiem, Achmat Meirah Sabera, Ahmed Ismail, Melvin Matthews, Dorothy Williams, Waheed Hartley, Paul Weinberg, Thessa Bos, Tessa Gordon, Mac McKenzie, Lalou Meltzer, Patricia Davidson, Gary Alter and the 214 Art Centre, George Hallet, Freddie Ogterroep, Lisba Vosloo, Vivian Bickford-Smith, Valmot Layne, Stephanie Gross, Megan Lovett, Alan Mabin, Cynthia Kros, Shamil Jeppie and Claudia Dos Santos.

John Edwin Mason
2010

Achmat Young and a junior member of the Pennsylvanians Crooning Minstrels

Anvar Hendricks

Eugene Johnson

Johnny Domingo

Franklin Edwards

Lazaan Jacobs

Lettie Toerien (left) and Maredia Abrahams (right)

Merle Jones

TOP The late Henry 'Gapie' van Aswyk with his wife
and granddaughter
BOTTOM 'Gapie' van Aswyk (left) and Abduragiem
'Giempie' Jacobs (right)
OPPOSITE Sedick Hoosain and Christel Gertze